Teaching Adolescents the Fundamentals of Life

A Guide to Living a Productive Lifestyle

James E. Puckett Sr.

ISBN: 978-1-80558-714-9 (Paperback)

ISBN: 978-1-80558-715-6 (Hardcover)

Printed in the United States of America

This book is dedicated to my grandchildren and great-grandchildren, to every young person who desires to live a quality life and contribute positively to society, and to the parents who want to see their children live a productive life.

Introduction

My main goal for writing this book is to help adolescents live a better quality of life. It is designed to empower parents, teens, and adolescents with the information they need to fundamentally change the way they live, from a life of self-destruction to a life of self-achievement.

The goal is to bring up a generation of adolescents that won't be influenced by external negative and immoral forces. This will enable them to become successful contributors in their homes, schools, communities, churches, and to the world. Don't be alarmed if you were never taught or even exposed to the topics and ideas presented in this book. Consider this as the first step on your journey to a new way of living. After you have read through this book from front to back, go back and review what you have read. Read it again and again, until you are informed, begin to reform, and sense a transformation happening in your life. You will begin to feel better about yourself, and others will begin to look at you in a different way, too.

What if every parent and young person who reads this book puts this information to work in his or her daily living? They just might help change the people and empower them to create a better way of living. So don't forget to tell your friends and family about this book. It's an opportunity for them to help change the world and bring some positive changes to their own lives as well.

His Servant,

James E. Puckett Sr.

Contents

My Personal Commentary

In past years, I have had the honor to work with and around some awesome teenagers I know their parents are proud of each of them. At the same time, I have worked with and around some less well-behaved young people. In this book, I will place my focus on the teens and adolescents of the present and future.

In my experience, many adolescents of this generation are rebellious, defiant, pernicious, and disrespectful. We live in a time when wrong is seen as right, right is seen as wrong, good is seen as bad, and bad is seen as good. As I watch people come and go in their daily living, it amazes me how evil and corrupt this society is. As I worked with and around teens, I was greatly concerned about where this great nation, the United States, is headed. As I travel about, watch television, listen to the radio, read the newspapers, and observe from other standpoints, I am disturbed by the actions and behaviors many of our young people are involved in. In my opinion, we are bringing up a generation of children where some of them seek to dominate their homes, their communities, and their schools. Until we as parents wake up and acknowledge that our children are being taught to live a self-destructive life, we will have the privilege of sharing in our children's self-destructive lifestyle. This is not just a local problem; it's nationwide.

The family unit that I grew up knowing has diminished; meanwhile, homes, communities, and schools are elevated with evil. In our present society, there has been a role reversal. Today, many teens control what goes on in the home. Many of them tell their parents what he or she is or is not going to do. When I grew up, this was the role and responsibility of the parents. Was the way families functioned back then all wrong? Is the way many families operate today, right? Personally, I'm glad I had someone to look after me, to tell me what was safe and unsafe, and to help me maneuver through this thing called life. If I had been allowed to do my own thing and make my own decisions, I would have gotten myself into jams that even my parents couldn't have gotten me out of. If parents are not raising their children today, then who—or what—is raising them? Children must be taught that there is a protocol for everything they choose to be involved in. Their conduct in life will be measured by the training they receive in their homes, at the hands of their parents. Contrary to popular belief, the home is the primary place to teach children. Schools are not responsible for teaching children how to behave, dress, or conduct themselves in public. Discipline starts at home. If children were all disciplined at home, then the schools wouldn't have to deal with so many behavior problems.

Today's technology has largely served to amplify poor behavior in teens. Now, I will be the first to admit that I love today's technology. I have a cell phone equipped with a camera and texting abilities. I own two laptop computers, which I can mobilize throughout the house. There are so many other good inventions that were meant to help mankind, but which have also turned out to be some of our biggest downfalls. Take the Internet for example, one can just about find anything that he or she is looking for. It is a great tool for researching and gathering information on just about any subject. One can post pictures and upload information to share with family and friends that live across the world. One can search for employment and even post one's resume. Looking up addresses and phone numbers has never been easier. Likewise, law enforcement personnel use the internet to track, catch, and convict criminals.

Like many other inventions, the computer was designed to improve our way of life. It has become part of our daily lives, and oftentimes, it can be addictive. The internet has also proved to be one of the worst, yet most effective tools at corrupting our teens, who use it as a way of degrading and insulting their peers through cyberbullying, posting foul language about teen gang violence, and sharing nude or sexually explicit pictures of themselves or others.

The cell phone is another tool invented to improve our lives. It was meant for healthy and moral communication purposes. But adolescents have taken the modern-day cell phone and turned it into a destructive tool. The use of cell phones in school has become one of the negative influences on students' ability to learn because it has become a major distraction in classrooms. Many students concentrate more on messaging their peers than they do on schoolwork. I believe that if students are allowed to have cell phones in school it should be for emergency purposes only. The cell phone should be off and out of sight and only taken out in case of an emergency. Some teens have discovered that they can send and receive both voice and text messages specifically designed to hurt their victims. In addition to the problems the internet and cell phones have caused, we cannot forget about television, movies, video games, and all the different apps used by young people with the same effects. Should we ignore these things and say, "These are just means of entertainment," or will we acknowledge that these can negatively influence our kids?

Computers and cell phones are not "bad" in and of themselves. The problem lies in how they are used to hurt, shame, and threaten others. These devices have a greater influence on children than on parents, teachers, administrators, or security personnel. Again I ask, who or what is teaching our children?

As I look at most adolescents and teens today, I wonder whom or what they are modeling their behavior and decisions after. A positive role model in the life of a child is very important. As I observe children, most of them view some celebrity figure as his or her role model. The problem with this is that some celebrities are not positive role models. Regardless, they are still able to exercise influence over our children as role models in some form or fashion. They all teach our children something, whether it's good or bad, right or wrong. Instead, our children need to be associated with people who will present themselves in a positive manner toward them. But be warned that a positive role model today can quickly change to a negative one tomorrow. We can only view role models by their current actions and behaviors.

I didn't always think this way, but now, I believe that parents should be their children's first role model, the first example he or she should look to. One would hope that the parents would be positive role models. As I've gotten older and wiser, I have realized the influence that my parents had on me as a child. Of course, in my younger years, I didn't view this as being important, but now that I'm married and have children, grandchildren, and great-grandchildren of my own, I understand the importance of having both a father and mother in the home and setting that positive example for children. When I think about the qualities of a role model, I think about someone who has integrity, honesty, loyalty, who is loving and hardworking, and who is a provider. As I look back on my childhood, I can see all this and more in my parents. My parents were my positive role models, and it was a choice that they both made, even though I didn't know it at the time. So, I say, "Thank you, Dad and Mom." I hope that one day, my kids can say the same things about me.

When it comes to teaching children what's right and what's wrong, it must be done with respect towards the child, and it must be done with consistency. Children must know and understand why something is considered right or wrong. I believe it's the parent's responsibility to teach his or her children the "whys" of right and wrong and to try to answer their questions and help them understand. I believe parents should give careful thought to this process beforehand. I have learned, both from working with and around children for many years and from my master's degree in counseling, that adolescents are less likely to reject information when it is shared as a part of small talk. This creates continuity in the relationship. Waiting until they make the wrong choice to teach them about right and wrong is a poor choice on the part of the parents. When parents choose to make small talk with their children, a bond develops between them, creating natural opportunities for open conversations. When a child makes the choice to break the law and ends up behind bars, it's a little too late to lecture them on drinking and driving, the company they keep, or other bad behaviors. Answering your children's "whys" in advance will help them make wise life choices when they are faced with uncertainties.

When parents fail to teach their children right from wrong, the children will come to their own conclusions about what is right or wrong based on their surroundings and on influences from others. Doing what's wrong doesn't just stem from wrong teaching; it can also come from a lack of teaching the right thing. Teaching young people to make the right choices is imperative in helping them avoid making false conclusions or destructive decisions about life and its challenges. When wrong conclusions are developed from a child's experiences, they will always have trouble distinguishing right from wrong. This is why I believe children must be informed as early as possible to be reformed and transformed in their ways of thinking and behaviors.

One may ask the question: "How early *is* as early as possible?" I remember as a little boy, still in diapers, I would get my little hands, legs, and behind slapped whenever I exercised any type of negative behavior. Did I understand why I was getting such attention at first? No! But if I continued my negative behavior, the slapping became more intense and forceful; consequently, over time, I learned that such behaviors would not be accepted—at least, not in the presence of my father and mother.

Just as children learn rules at a young age, they also learn how to manipulate their parents and others early in life so they can get their way. Many small children are pros at redirecting their parents' attempts to deny them what they want. Children who receive overwhelming attention through poor behavior, without any negative consequences, quickly learn how far they can go and what it takes to get their way.

I have witnessed young children in public places, some still in their training pants and barely able to walk, use the word "no" to reject something their parents had just told them. The child knows to make such a fuss that the parents give in, reinforcing the child's methods of using poor behavior to get their way. I watch and listen, thinking, "If these children are not corrected *now*, they will grow up displaying the same negative behavior; perhaps with an even more forceful approach to get their way."

So, when is "as early as possible" exactly? It depends on the child and the environment. I believe correction and parental intervention should begin as soon as there are signs of negative behaviors. If a small child is old enough to form the word "no" in their mind and speak it aloud, then I believe they are also capable of understanding why they are saying it and what they expect to gain from it.

A few years ago, I was volunteering at one of the local public elementary schools. I was working with a first grader as his lunch buddy once a week. This young child was very intelligent, but he had one problem—he didn't like to be told no. At home and at school, he would have meltdowns every time someone told him no. His parents and his teachers all knew that intervention was needed quickly. One day, the school counselor approached me and asked me if I could help him understand that being told "No" is part of life. I agreed, but I really didn't know what I was getting myself into.

The next week, when I went to have lunch with him and after some small talk, I went right into the issue he was having. What I learned from this five-year-old was something we as grownups struggle with from time to time. He was convinced that when he was told "no," he was being picked on and that nobody cared about what mattered to him. He was only focused on the negative result of a "No." He simply could not comprehend the positive side of being told "No."

I realized that this was going to be a challenging task. I had one week before I was scheduled to meet with this child again. During that time, I prayed and asked God for wisdom on how to help him. Over the next several months, while trying to explain why he must be told "no" at times, his behavior was not improving, and at times, seemed to be getting worse. A few weeks later, his school went on Christmas break. This is when God gave me the idea of my children's book, *The Kid Who Didn't Like to Be Told* No, which has become a bestseller amongst parents and grandparents with small children. I quickly wrote the book and had it published. After getting approval to share it with my little lunch buddy, we went through the book page by page and discussed the positives of being told "no." It didn't take long for my five-year-old friend to catch on.

To him, being told "no" was like being told he wasn't important, and that those people didn't care about him. All children like him need is for someone to explain to them why they are or are not allowed to do certain things. It could be for many reasons, but they need to be told. For this five-year-old, God used me to share a story with him in the form of a book.

Too often, we as parents look at this type of negative behavior and do not give it serious thought because the child is so small. We may even find it funny at times. However, children recognize this response, and, over time, they will also find humor in their own negative behavior. The more laughs and attention they get for negative behavior, the more frequent and intense the behavior becomes.

I am concerned that today's average family unit has allowed the pendulum of its child's behavior to go too far to the left or right. Even children need to be taught that there is a balance to life. I believe that too much exposure to one thing and not enough to others will teach a child what is viewed as acceptable and unacceptable. If a child is allowed to grow up exposed to too much of the way the world lives, their life will consist of the same. Allowing children to be exposed to certain types of things too early will infect their minds, which could lead to self-destruction later. This is why I believe it is vitally important that parents start to teach their children as early as possible. The more opportunities a child has to explore what society offers, without regulation, the harder it becomes to reach them. I am not suggesting that parents should try and shield their children from normal experiences, but I do believe that parents ought to monitor what their children are exposed to and should teach them that balance is necessary for a healthy lifestyle.

No parent or grandparent wants their children to grow up and live a self-destructive lifestyle, but sadly, many do. A child is born into this world knowing nothing. If parents fail to teach their children about right and wrong while they are young, this leaves them to discover things on their own, which could cause them to self-destruct later. The child will go through life, however long that is, causing chaos not only in their life but in the lives of those around them.

Chapter One
Developing Respect for Authority

Having respect for something or someone will determine how you react to that something or that someone. Showing respect for a person, whether directly, or showing respect for someone else that person represents, will make life much better for us all. Respect in general is one thing that is lacking amongst many people of all ages in our present society, but in particular, the lack of respect for authority from many teenagers today is growing at an alarming rate. In my opinion, this has caused some major behavior problems in schools across the nation.

Before we go any further, I also want to caution you upfront about something. When I talk about having respect for people in uniform or those with titles, I am not suggesting that the people in these positions should become so arrogant and prideful that they can go around demanding respect. In my opinion, people who have earned the right to wear a uniform or add a title to their name are worthy of a baseline of respect in their specialty. So, hear me loud and clear, being arrogant and full of self-pride about yourself will get you no respect. Titles and positions can be stripped from a person far more quickly than the time it took to earn them.

Showing respect for a person (or the person he or she represents) can set one's life on a course of victories. I see respect as one of the foundational principles for living a successful life. Showing respect where respect is due adds years of quality life to one's soul. Just respecting others for who they are will cause you to think well about them. Respecting others and what they stand for will help one control the emotions and feelings that might come. Showing disrespect where respect is due is like a heart suffering from an abnormal beat. As we disrespect people and things that are worthy of respect, we start to lose a portion of our lives. When this happens, we begin to live an abnormal life, which eventually leads to an even more destructive pattern.

Respect is a foundational principle for life, and it is something that is taught; it is not self-learned, as some would believe. No one can learn what respect is on their own. One may learn what respect looks like, or the actions behind it, but only after he or she has been taught. What does respect look like or act like? Below are just a few of the things I believe represent a person operating in respect.

- Respect is opening the door for someone.
- Respect is allowing the other person to go first.
- Respect is giving a gift when appropriate.
- Respect is not always having one's way.
- Respect is defending the person you call a friend.
- Respect is seeking peace in the midst of adversity.
- Respect is not prejudging a person, action, or situation before one has all the facts.
- Respect is acknowledging the opinions of others.
- Respect is keeping your hands to yourself.

Learning those kinds of respect was the result of someone applying some sort of teaching technique to you, whether direct or indirect. Unfortunately, the society we live in today teaches more disrespect than respect. Society has camouflaged evil to appear as good and wrong to appear as right. When this happens, how can any level of respect for anyone or anything be granted? Respect is lost in the hands of a disrespectful, ungrateful society.

Respect not only has action behind it, but it also says something. Respect speaks. What does respect say?

- Respect says, "I am sorry."
- Respect says, "Forgive me."
- Respect says, "Excuse me."

- Respect says, "I love you."
- Respect says, "I am proud of you."
- Respect says, "Please."
- Respect says, "You look nice today."
- Respect says, "Allow me."
- Respect says, "Thank you."
- Respect says, "I appreciate you."

Respect says only those things that show honor, compassion, and reverence to a person, thing, or cause. Again, all of these things are taught. They are taught in one of two ways: either by example or by instruction. A pilot is taught to fly a plane by another pilot who has already been taught how to fly a plane. After the teacher (the flight instructor) has taught a series of lessons on the mechanics of flying the plane, they will transition to teaching through "doing," or as it is better known, "hands-on teaching."

Children must have an example of respect to model their own behavior after. Parents are their children's first example when it comes to teaching respect. Parents teach their children through doing and by instructing them. Children are taught by what they observe in their parents. They will do what they see their parents doing and say what they hear their parents saying. But children will not necessarily do what their parents tell them to do (or not do) just because they say to do it. Instead, they will copy what they see and hear their friends doing and saying. Likewise, children will do and say the things that their society dictates. Essentially, children learn from their parents, friends, or the media.

Children can also be taught respect by a mentor, and this is something I strongly believe in. But first, the children must be willing to be accountable to someone who is superior to him or her, and they must respect the mentor as someone who has either gone where they desire to go or done what they desire to do. If accountability in the mentor relationship is missing, the mentorship will not work. Second, if the child is not willing to be corrected during the relationship, the mentorship will fail. I would suggest that with the approval of the parents, adolescents seek out someone other than their parents who they can be mentored by—someone they can look up to and respect. It will produce much fruit later in their lives.

I believe that every adolescent should have someone in his or her life who they can not only learn from but who they can also receive advice and correction from. However, I am not suggesting that parents allow their children to be mentored by just anyone. The mentor must be a trusted person: a best friend, a family member, or an authority figure. These can all make very good mentors. Parents should always have knowledge of whom their children are getting advice and correction from; likewise, children should also be taught not to take advice and correction from just anyone. Common sense should be used in choosing a mentor. Teachers, administrators, counselors, and coaches are usually good choices, but these also should be filtered through the parents. Parents should always be first in line to offer their children mentorship.

Early in my military career, I became interested in becoming a warrant officer. Warrant officers are highly respected and possess special skills in specific areas. During my first assignment in Germany, I positioned myself to become a "mentee" to a warrant officer in my unit, but not just any warrant officer. I chose the one who I believed had the skills, knowledge, and expertise that matched what I was interested in becoming. In fact, I was being mentored by him long before he knew who I was. Whenever possible, I would watch his every move, listen to how he communicated with his subordinates and superiors, and study his leadership style. It wasn't that I wanted to do or say things *exactly* the way he did, but I did want to model myself after his conduct. He illustrated his character not just in talk but also demonstrated it in his walk. It was important that I learned the proper way for warrant officers to conduct themselves.

I then made it my business to get to know him on a personal level. No, we didn't hang out together or visit one another at our living quarters, but when I was at work, I would make it my business to be around him. I would ask him questions about his job and about his responsibilities as a warrant officer. He was my mentor, but he never knew it. Maybe he thought I was just being curious or nosey, but in fact, he was teaching me how to show respect and how to be respected.

For me, this warrant officer was the first of many warrant officer mentors over the next 24+ years. As a rookie, I needed all the help I could get, and it was up to me to seek it from senior warrant officers in the same career field. I had to be willing to submit myself to some strong advice and some tough correction at times. This taught me how to relate to both my subordinates and to my superiors in uniform. Their teachings made me humble in what I did and taught me to show humility to those I worked for. When I look back, I can say with complete honesty that it was all worth it. The things I learned from those men helped me become, maintain, and eventually retire from the distinguished rank of Chief Warrant Officer Four (CWO4). It was with the help of their mentorship that I had a successful career in the United States Army.

I believe that any parent who cares about and loves their child will try to teach them good moral ethics to live by. I believe that many parents with adolescent children are doing their best to teach and instruct them to do the right thing. But the challenge many parents face is the fact that they must compete with an immoral society. The media and all its teachings and instructions are poisoning our children. The teachings and instructions of the parents are less effective on the child, whereas the teachings and instructions of the society—media, television, video games, movies, internet, handheld electronic devices, and many others—are very effective. Believe it or not, society is teaching and instructing our children more than we may know or realize.

Train Yourself Through Practice

Practice! Practice! Practice! Military people, past and present, are some of the most respected people in the world. I served for almost 25 years in the military. What I learned about my job was through teaching and practice. Someone had to teach me what I was required to know. After I received the teaching, it was all about practice and more practice. Even when you thought you had made every move correctly or executed every order to the letter, more practice was always needed. Practice takes discipline on the part of the one being taught. Practice can take place in either a group or an individual setting. Both are effective, but in my experience, individual practice teaches self-discipline and respect for oneself and others more than group practice.

Both enlisted and officers of all ranks deserve the utmost respect. During my first year, I was taught to always respect rank and uniform. Certain ranks required respect by rendering a salute, while others required a greeting. Before I learned all the officer-level ranks, it was sometimes a challenge to determine what person in uniform was worthy of a salute. As an enlisted soldier, you are required to salute all officers; it is not optional. At times, it was difficult to recognize a rank, enlisted or officer, from a distance. As a private, you were taught to live by the principle of, "When in doubt, whip it out." Meaning, if you were unsure whether the soldier in uniform you were approaching was due honor and respect by saluting, you should err on the side of caution and salute just in case. By putting this principle into practice, I saved myself a bunch of chew-outs.

Later in my career, I became a non-commissioned officer, and later, a warrant officer. It wasn't until then that I fully understood why the "rank" was so worthy of respect. I am speaking of both enlisted and officer ranks. Certain achievements were required in order to advance to the next rank. Remember, we are not taking anything away from the uniform, because it receives respect all by itself. Every person that is required to wear a uniform to carry out his or her assigned daily duties has earned the right to be respected. Will people always respect these uniforms? No, they will not! But I believe that being obedient when it comes to respect is the first step in becoming a leader. I would never have earned a leadership position in the military if I had taken respect lightly.

While attending the Warrant Officer Candidate School, I had an experience that I will never forget. On my first day of school, the entire class was put under extreme pressure at the hands of our instructors, the "tact officers." I am not sure why they called themselves tact officers, because I never found anything tactful about them while I was training there. But on this day, our class was ordered to move from one building to another. The upstairs class moved from one building to the downstairs building next to it, while the downstairs class moved the other way, from the downstairs to the upstairs building. We only had a certain amount of time to complete this task. Imagine a total of 40 enlisted soldiers, all non-commissioned officers, running and scrambling up and down flights of stairs from one building to another. Everywhere you turned there was a tact officer screaming and yelling something in your ears. It was total confusion and chaos that morning.

That very same morning, I missed an important opportunity to train myself to be respectful through practice. Because of all the pressure I was under, I said a curse word and one of the tact officers heard me. Because of my disrespect for the rank, the position, and to whom I was a representative, I was entertained by several tact officers and a very intimidating first sergeant for twenty minutes or more. I became the target subject of their instructions because I let one word of disrespect slip out. I missed it. I had known what I should have done but had failed to do it because I let the pressure and stress get to me.

My point in telling you this story is to warn you that there will come a time when you will be under pressure and stress when someone or something will require that you show respect. Take it from me, it is better to render respect up front in all situations. If someone fails to show respect to law enforcement, he or she will usually be sorry they didn't. Show disrespect in Judge Judy's courtroom, and you and your case will be kicked out.

Then there are those who are not required to wear a uniform, but who are also worthy of respect by virtue of their title or position. Consider the President of the United States, members of Congress, senators, governors, pastors, teachers, administrators, counselors, fathers, mothers, grandparents, uncles, and aunts. These people don't normally wear a uniform while carrying out their daily duties, but because of their title or position, they are worthy of respect. At some point in their journey to success, they were taught and trained in the importance of respect and were challenged to practice respect toward others. They sowed respect, and now respect is also reaped.

Again, I want to emphasize the importance of all young people showing respect for authority, but I wanted to first take the opportunity to lay a good foundation for what I wanted to say. Respect is an area that many adolescents are lacking today; respect in the family is diminishing at an alarming rate. Because of this, teens don't have a model to pattern themselves after in their future lives. I write these things openly and hope I don't offend anyone because that is not my intention.; but I am concerned about the direction our children are headed.

My intention is to inform the young generation and their parents that this fundamental, foundational principle must be brought back into every home around the world: respect for authority. Every person graced with life must be taught how to give respect to living a successful, productive life. No one person is exempted from it.

Respect must be shown and taught in the family. The husband must respect his wife and her wishes. The wife must respect her husband and his wishes. The children must respect their parents as the authority figures in the home and respect the rules of the house. The parents must, as much as possible, respect their children. Not to the extent that they allow their children to do whatever they want, or go wherever they desire, but respect that they have intelligent minds and can think, and most of all that they are each a person created by God, the same as their parents. I believe the most important way parents can respect their children is by providing them with the necessities of life and making sure they are safe. That includes providing them with teaching and modeling of what respect looks like, what it acts like, and what it says.

Simply teaching a child what is right and wrong is good, but it will not, in my opinion, accurately prepare them for their life's journey. Children must be taught to intentionally practice skills if the skills are to have long-lasting effects on their lives. If respect is not taught in the home, the child will lack one of the main ingredients for success. He or she will never learn how to earn respect if it was never taught to them. Respect that is taught at the hands of the law is much harder on both the child and the parents. So, if all else fails at home, train yourself through practice. Let respect be a major part of your behavioral pattern. Respect is taught and practiced until it is built into one's mentality. A good place to start is at home. Parents should be viewed as the authority figures they are. Parents should require that their children practice respect towards them and the community. Parents are the leaders in the home. All people in leadership positions are to be treated with respect. I am told that it takes 14-21 days of repetitive behavior to form a new habit in the brain, which then becomes an automatic behavior habit. Let today be your first day in this process.

Seize the First Opportunity

For many years, I worked with and around teenagers daily as a school resource officer (SRO). During that time, I experienced firsthand the lack of respect many adolescents and teens have toward authority.

Many of the situations that involved teenagers I was asked to assist with were because they had failed to show respect at the first opportunity. Many of those situations could have been avoided if only the student had done what he or she was asked by the person of authority, in those cases, a teacher or administrator. I am not suggesting that my appearance would make him or her jump to attention. Many times, once the students set their eyes on me, their behavior became more aggressive. Why is this? Didn't they know that their teacher is a person of authority? Didn't they know that the administrators are people of authority? Didn't they know that if security must be called in, things have gone too far? Did they care? Why did these teenagers allow something as simple as handing over a cell phone to a teacher to develop into out-of-school suspension (OSS)? After all, school policy clearly states: "No use of cell phones in the classrooms."

Some teenagers don't care about school rules and policies. They seem to think that rules and policies are for everyone but them. Just think about all the people in authority they failed to respect because of a cell phone. They disrespected their teacher, administrator, parents, school board members, school security, and themselves. Respecting the school policy by not using a cell phone during class could have avoided the whole incident. If they had honored the teacher's request and handed over the cell phone, the most that would have happened is that the cell phone would have been turned over to administration for their parents to pick up. But instead, they chose to make a mountain out of a molehill.

Could this be why the child had no desire or wish to obey the first or second request? Could it be that they knew their parents would side with them? Could it be that they knew there would be no consequences from their parents for their actions? Could it be that because respect was never taught in the home the child didn't know what respect acted like?

Another area where I see respect is lacking in our society and schools is the way adolescents and teens address people in positions of authority. I must take you back to my childhood days to give you an illustration of what I mean. This is an example of what respect would say when a child would address an adult. It did not matter if he or she was in a position of authority or not. You were taught to address a man as "Mr." or "Sir," and a woman as "Madam," "Miss" or "Mrs." That was it. Period! No other names were acceptable when talking to a person who was older than you or in a position of authority.

In my family, children were taught to respond to our parents with "Yes, sir" and "No, sir," or "Yes, madam" and "No, madam." It was the same with my grandparents, adult neighbors, adults at church, and adults in the community. I was taught to address all adults in these same ways. First and last names alone were off-limits. If my father or mother witnessed one of their children using an adult's first or last name alone, they quickly corrected us.

Because we were taught to talk like this in the home, when we were challenged with showing respect in public, we seized the first opportunity. Nowadays, talking like that is like speaking a foreign language to most adolescents and teens I encountered during my time working as a school security officer.

When I was attending elementary, middle, and high school, addressing a teacher or administrator by their first or last name alone would result in some sort of punishment. Respect was given to teachers and administrators by addressing them as "Mr." or "Ms." and "Mrs." Using only the first name or last name, as many students today do, would be considered disrespectful. When I was working as a school security officer, every time I witnessed students addressing teachers and administrators by their first or last name, I would correct them. Why? I believe it's because I was taught as a child that this was the respectful thing to do. I would always address teachers and administrators with the respect he or she had earned no matter what their age. It was simply done to honor the position or title.

As a uniformed officer, one would think that respect would be granted by all students encountered. Not so in this society. Many of the students I have worked with and around don't know what it means to show respect to a uniformed officer. I have experienced this in both middle and high school. For example, the way some of them would react when I confronted them about a situation, and the words that came out of their mouth, would sometimes cause me to take a step backward. Their whole demeanor and body language would spell "disrespect."

At times, I was called everything but "officer" by many students. Often, I would ask myself, "What did I do to cause this student to react in such a disrespectful manner?" The only justifiable answer would be that he or she was never taught what respect looks like, acts like, or sounds like. If respect had been taught to them in the home, the students would have seized the opportunity when I first approached them.

I cannot remember having any type of uniformed officers present when I attended elementary, middle, or high school. I believe that during that time, children were so afraid of their parents and teachers that school security was not needed. I know for myself that if I had gotten into trouble, I had to face my parents. Not to suggest that I was a saint of some sort, but back then children showed more respect for people in positions of authority, including their parents. Respect and reverence toward my parents were the two main reasons that kept me out of major trouble. Disrespecting someone in a position of authority would be like disrespecting the entire family, and sometimes, the entire community.

As a child in our home, I was taught that law enforcement personnel were to be feared. Not feared in a bad way but feared in the sense of viewing them with reverence and respect. I was taught that because of their position or title, I should show respect and honor for their badge, uniform, and what their duties meant. Just the word "police" had a dramatic, positive effect on how I would behave. Some people get nervous when they are driving down the road and a police officer or state trooper's car drives up behind them. They check their speed and are careful about making sure they don't sway back and forth from right to left. Likewise, teens should show the same respect to people in authority, especially to parents, teachers, administrators, and law enforcement personnel.

I remember a time when I was working at this high school that was hosting a sporting event. I witnessed a parent who missed a grand opportunity to teach her child a lesson in respecting authority. Her child was stopped by me as he attempted to wander into a restricted area, which was clearly marked by wooden sawhorses that had been painted bright yellow and had bold, black letters that read, **"DO NOT ENTER**." The student insisted that he be allowed to go past it and became very disrespectful toward me.

At this point, his mother approached and asked him what was wrong. He told her that I wouldn't allow him to go to his locker. The mother looked at me and said, "Why can't my son go to his locker?" I explained why. She then gave me a dirty look, turned, and said, "I have never seen a school with so many rules. I hate this school." She and her son then left the building.

She said these things in that manner in front of her son, and yet we wonder why some of our children act and talk the way that they do. Imagine a parent behaving in such a disrespectful manner in the presence of her child. This parent, whether she realized it or not, was teaching her child how to disrespect authority. I believe this child, on that night, behaved in the same manner he does at home. I believe he disrespects his parents the same way he disrespected me. Remember the first grader I told you about who didn't like to be told "no?" Well, this student was in the eleventh grade. This is why I said, "Respect is taught." Despite his age, this child had never been taught to respect, or at the very least, not to respect laws, rules, and policies. He clearly proved it that night. You could properly conclude that his mother didn't know or care much about respect for authority either because she didn't seize the opportunity to use the situation as a teaching opportunity for her son.

I am reminded of another incident that occurred at a different sporting event at which I was working. I approached two females and asked them to stop a certain behavior because it could have created a safety hazard. After getting their attention, it was clear to me from their body language that it was going to be a challenge. Once I was sure I had their attention, I began to make my request to them. I started the conversation with, "Excuse me, madam," followed by, "Would you please," and then followed by my request. Neither of them was willing to do what I asked them to do.

It wasn't as if someone in street clothes had approached them and asked them to do something. I was in my duty uniform. Everyone could clearly see why I was there in that building. Neither one of these women could have mistaken me for someone who was not on duty as a safety and security officer. It was just pure disrespect on their part, and they stopped at nothing to get their way. Both women had a few choice words for me and continued to refuse to do what I asked them to do. They both continued to verbally abuse me and cause a commotion. I knew that if I allowed this behavior to continue, everyone in the building would be affected by their acts of disrespect. At this point, I ordered the older of the two to leave the building, which she refused to do.

To make a long story short, the woman ended up being arrested by the local authorities after she refused to obey all verbal orders given to her. This lady turned out to be the mother of the other woman. I was shocked to learn that this was a mother behaving this way in front of her daughter.

Why is it that some people think they can do whatever they want and expect to get away with it? Why is it so hard for some people to just do the right thing? Why do some parents teach their children to behave in such a rebellious, defiant, pernicious, and disrespectful manner? *No parent would do such a terrible thing*, you are probably thinking. Or, you might be saying, "She didn't teach her child to behave that way." You might be right. But she didn't teach her child *not* to behave that way. The negative behavior is by default. Whether she was aware of it or not, this is exactly what this mother was doing. Her daughter got a course in Disrespect 101, taught by her mother. However, I suspect she had taught his lesson several times before—some of the same words that came from the mother's mouth also came from the daughter's mouth. A level of anger was also expressed by both women. I will discuss anger in further detail later in this book.

Like the scenario with the young man, this mother also missed an opportunity to teach her daughter how to look, act, and speak with respect. Instead, she chose to go to jail. Several other adolescents and teens were also subjected to her verbally and physically abusive behavior. Just a little bit of respect for authority would have prevented this whole incident.

There have been many times, I have stood and watched people get out of their cars and move orange traffic cones so they could drive through, only to discover that a locked gate awaited them. Then I watch them get out of their car to check if the gate is locked. Once they discover the gate is locked, they express anger and disappointment, get back in their car, turn around, and proceed in the direction they should have gone to begin with. The cones were placed there to let motorists know that there was no exit and to proceed in a certain direction. These people disrespected objects that plainly warned them that the area was off-limits. It makes me wonder if these same people will disrespect stop signs, traffic lights, or posted speed limits. And not one of these people took the time to place the cones back where they found them. They all missed several opportunities to exercise respect and put it into practice. I believe that people who violate such laws somehow think that the laws don't apply to them—the cones were set up for someone else, not them, just like the young man assumed the sawhorses were placed there just for people who choose to respect authority and obey laws.

Every person is at the point in his or her life where they can seize their first opportunity to show respect if they have never done so in the past. I believe it is vitally important for people of all ages, especially children, to start as early as possible, because the longer a child rebels against respecting his or her parents and authority figures altogether, the harder it is to change later in life.

Obey Your Boundaries in Life

Adolescents must be taught that in their life's journey, they will be held to a set of boundaries. They must understand that some things and places are prohibited. Boundaries are normally set to protect themselves as well as others. Children must be taught boundaries in the home, which will then extend to the community, school, and into their future lives. One wouldn't cross the centerline into oncoming traffic while driving! The line was placed there as a tool to let drivers know what side of the road to drive on in order to maintain their safety and the safety of others.

Just as in the sports of basketball, football, and other sports, there are boundary lines. These lines are drawn to help each player stay within the boundaries of the area of play and abide by the rules of the game. If a player with the ball steps out of bounds while he or she is in possession of the ball, while running a play, the game is temporarily stopped, and the ball is given to the other team. Likewise, when you and I disobey the boundaries set before us and around us, our life is temporarily halted or slowed down. Sometimes, the consequence can even be death.

If any adolescent has doubts about whether boundaries are real, they should visit their local correction facility. At some place and at some point, each person behind bars went past his or her established boundaries. Each one of them did something or went somewhere that had been established as being off-limits to them. They failed to respect the laws that they were governed by. Failing to respect boundaries in life can land a person behind bars, or even worse, result in them ending up dead.

Everyone has boundaries they must obey, but each one of us will be held to different boundaries. Just because one person is allowed to go to a certain place or do a certain thing, does not mean another will not be restricted. Boundaries in one's life journey can change as the person grows, matures, and learns to be responsible. But there are certain boundaries that every person is bound to for his or her entire life. As we think about the laws we are subject to, we can recognize these as the boundaries that every person must not go past.

Likewise, children should have boundaries in their homes. They should know what boundaries are set and what they mean. They should know the consequences of failure to obey these boundaries. This will prepare them for the boundaries they will face in the community, school, and later in life. Teens must understand that they will always be required to function within a set of boundaries. Where they attend school is no exception. Every day, school administrators, teachers, and school security work hard to keep schools safe. For them to be effective at their jobs, keeping students within their boundaries must be a priority. Every student must understand and acknowledge that boundaries are set in place to protect them and to keep them from going out of bounds and having to face the consequences, such as having some or all of their freedom taken away.

Once I was preparing for a large sporting event that was scheduled to take place at the high school where I worked when something surprising happened to me. I was making my way around the sports complex, putting yellow security tape around places that would be restricted to students and everyone in attendance at the event. The yellow security tape was marked with black bold letters "**Security Line, Do Not Cross**." I had just finished taping off an area when a parent, who was also making preparations for the upcoming sporting event that night, approached me and asked if it was ok for her to pass the security tape to gather some items that she had left sitting next to a building. I was blown away by her question. I was shocked that she would even bother to ask permission. First, she took the time to locate me and approach me, and second, she explained that she didn't want to enter the area that I had just taped as off-limits.

Of course, I gladly gave her permission and thanked her for asking. She began to tell me that she understood that the security tape was there for a reason. I also learned that her parents had taught her as a small child to obey laws and rules. She shared with me what would happen to her if she went against the boundaries that her parents had set for her as a child. I began to share with her how I wished that everyone had been taught about obeying boundaries set before them.

What this parent made me realize was this: even though the security tape did not speak to her in an audible voice, it brought back what she had been taught as a small child by her parents. She not only acknowledged what the security tape meant, but she acted on it. She didn't learn that something as simple as security tape meant no entry, she was *taught* this. This is more proof to make my case that respect (and obedience) should be taught in the home beginning as a small child.

Every day, you and I have opportunity after opportunity to obey boundaries set before us. Over the years, I have learned that there are places and things that I simply don't want to be involved in. In my lifetime, I have learned that putting up my own boundaries in life has kept me out of trouble. Just like we should seize the first opportunity to practice respect, we should also seize the first opportunity to practice the principle of obeying the boundaries set before you in life.

Respect for Others Starts with Having Respect for Oneself

Before one can be taught to show respect for others, it is imperative that one is taught to have respect for oneself. I believe that this is one of the main reasons children react in such a negative way when people in authority approach them. Teaching a child to have respect for oneself is done in the home. Parents are responsible for both telling and showing their children that they are valued and can grow up to be positive contributors to society. It is important that a child be taught that he or she is unique and possesses a special talent that is different from anyone else around him or her.

Many times, adolescents will look at others in their age group and desire to have the same or similar talents or gifts as their friends or acquaintances. A child must be taught to understand and accept that the talent and gift he or she has is unique to his or her personality. They must be taught that someone else may be just as talented or gifted in a similar area, and maybe even better at it, but each person can improve his or her gifts and talents by doing simple things such as reading, getting involved, and asking questions. If teens are taught to take whatever gift or talent they have and develop it through activity, their ability to do it well will increase. I believe this is important to the development of self-respect.

The reality is that not every child has the luxury of growing up in a home where self-respect is taught. Many adolescents live in environments where everything *but* respect for oneself is taught. Many times, young people are told how bad they are or how they will never amount to anything during their lifetime. This type of teaching will lead children to disrespect themselves. Saying negative things to children about their individual ability to accomplish certain things in life before they have even had the opportunity to try can leave them with a negative feeling about their ability to do anything right in life.

Whatever adolescents are told, either by words or through the actions of others, they will remember it for the rest of their lives. In many cases, this is where the positive mental growth of teens stops. This is why many children have problems with authority. All of their life, they hear nothing but negative and put-down words, and then when they are confronted with the words or actions of authority, they react to it by being disrespectful. If they have respect for themselves, however, then dealing with people in authority would not be as much of an issue. I am not suggesting that people in authority are always right, but in settings such as schools, every child's responsibility is to submit to authority and hash out any disagreements later.

Respecting the Property of Others

Children must be taught to respect what belongs to others. It doesn't matter how pretty it looks to them or how badly they want it; if it doesn't belong to them, they have no right to it. I know this may sound elementary to some, but it happens with children every day. I witnessed it when I was working in the school system, and I still witness it today. There are some children who think they can touch, grab, and hold objects that appeal to them. Granted, there are places where this kind of action is appropriate. For example, if you are attending a petting zoo and it's deemed by the staff as safe to pet the animals or some other activity where hands-on interaction is encouraged. Otherwise, it should be hands-off. In scenarios where permission is given, then respect for the property must be a high priority. It is the responsibility of the parents to teach their children to respect the property of others.

I was at a book signing inside a local grocery store when the unthinkable happened. I had my book table set up, and my books were all displayed neatly on the table. A copy of each one of my books was placed on a book stand for easy visibility to the patrons, and the remaining books were stacked neatly in front of them. When people came to the table and were interested in a particular one, many of them would ask if it was alright to look inside. I always gave them permission. They would remove the book from the top and place it back once they were finished. Most of the time, this is how it played out when people came to my table.

On this day, I had a family with two young children visit my table. The male child looked to be around six or seven years old and the female a little younger. I assumed they were siblings. As they approached, both the boy and girl went for my children's book, almost fighting to see who could grab it first. Three of the five book stands were knocked over, and books were scattered all over the table. I stood there in shock asking myself, "What just happened? Where are the parents of these children?" At this point, I was feeling a little defensive about what to say to these children. Their father is standing there watching all this happen and does not stop them. All I could say was, "No, no," and begin to upright the book stands, and place the books back in some sort of organization. As I was reorganizing the table, the children were still reaching for the books, and their dad said, "Kids, what are you doing?" The boy said, looking at the books. The dad never told them to stop or apologize. Shortly after, their mother walked over, and they went to grab the children's book again, knocking over the stand it was resting on. I was happy to see them leave—and, no, they didn't purchase a book. I didn't mind them looking at the books, but I also did not want them destroying my display.

Earlier, we talked about boundaries. This would have been a good place for these parents to teach their children about boundaries. But I suppose that was the way they acted everywhere they went. It's more difficult to try and teach a child right from wrong when he is in the act than it would be before he engages in the act. It's a bit too late to tell Little Johnny that running through a crowded store is dangerous after he has run into someone's cart and is now on the floor bleeding from a head wound. Little Johnny should have been taught this at home before he ever came to the store. If children are taught to have respect for other people and their property, an imaginary line would flash before their eyes telling them not to touch, grab, or handle in any way something that doesn't belong to them.

It was clear to me that these two kids didn't understand having respect for others or for their property. So, I concluded that not only were they not being taught this at home, but also, it didn't appear to be high on the parents' list of priorities at the time. I often ask myself, "At what stage of development should children start to understand the concept of boundaries to avoid fostering a sense of entitlement that can lead to an unhealthy lifestyle?"

Chapter Two
Anger Is a Deal Breaker?

More and more children of all ages are living with some sort of anger problem. Many are enrolled in anger management programs of some type or another, or even on medication to help them control their anger. Why are there so many children today living with such anger? How did this anger develop? And how can we help children combat it so they can live a normal life?

Over the years, I have witnessed more and more adolescents and teens dealing with anger. I have even been at the receiving end of some serious anger outbursts. I ask myself, why is this becoming the norm among so many children and young people? They haven't even started to live life yet. What in the world is making them so angry at everyone and everything around them? This tendency to anger affects all children: those who grow up in homes with both parents present as well as those in single-parent homes. It affects children born into wealthy families as much as it affects those raised in poverty.

I believe that the common denominator for the anger between all these children is a lack of structure in the home. Structure is important in all our lives. Without it, we would experience insecurity in everything we do. But with structure comes stability. Stability means that one has a solid grounding for his or her daily living. There must be stability in both a person's mind and actions. But structure and stability are not possible without a firm foundation. The foundation is what keeps stability and structure alive and standing. This is another reason I believe children must be taught early in life. Establishing this stability provides them with a proper foundation, which they will need to both work through any problem in the future and to live a productive life. I encourage you to read my award-winning book, *A God-Balanced Life*, in which I go into detail about maintaining stability in our lives. I believe that children who possess an anger problem lack a strong foundation of stability in their homes. Children who lash out at their parents, teachers, administrators, and others in authority mainly do so due to a lack of structure in their early lives.

Neglecting to give our children the right and proper foundation during their childhood years is like building a house without the footers. There is nothing to stabilize it when the strong winds and storms eventually crash against it. A builder starts from the bottom and works his way to the top, and there is a reason for this process: it is to make sure the house or structure has what it takes to stand in opposition to storms. A house built on a weak foundation can be easily destroyed with little or no effort—even the removal of one brick or one two-by-four could cause the whole structure to fall. Likewise, our children need a foundation, built through teaching and love, while they are still small, and that teaching and love must be continued throughout their adolescent and teenage years. The foundational years require a lot of love, care, and provision for children; this is imperative if they are to go through life without lashing out in anger when things don't go their way or when they don't agree with something.

It goes without saying that a child is not capable of taking care of him or herself. Children are not mature enough to make major decisions for their lives on their own; this is the role of their parents, who must make these decisions for them whether they are young children or older adolescents. However, when children are forced to make decisions for themselves on the necessities of life, they develop anger, simply because nothing seems to be working out in their favor. Children were not meant to provide for themselves. This is the responsibility of parents. When children start playing the role of parents, there is frustration and instability that develop and quickly turn into anger. Nothing goes right for them, and it cannot, because they are not developed enough to make those types of decisions at such a young age.

Wealthy children who are allowed to make their own decisions, who get their own way about nearly everything, and who never hear "No," are also likely to develop anger problems. On the other hand, children growing up in poverty who are forced to survive by stealing or even dealing drugs also develop serious anger problems. In both cases, the children grow up in homes without the structure or stability that is necessary for a solid foundation for life.

When these children are placed in environments where they are required to be under authority, such as in schools and community centers, they break down and lash out in anger. Anger becomes their defense mechanism. Up to this point in their lives, there has been very little to no authority—an element that is vital for a solid and firm way of living.

At one of the schools where I worked, there was a student who used to pass by me every morning. The reason he was so noticeable is that he was always late for class every morning. Every day, I would say, "Good morning," to this young man, and every day, he would just look at me with overwhelming anger on his face and in his eyes. This went on for about two months, until finally one morning, he responded with, "What's so good about it? I am always late." When I asked him why, he replied, "I must take care of my grandmother every morning before I come to school. I must feed her and give her medicine because she is dying from cancer." All I could say was, "I am sorry about your grandmother." This teenager was forced to do something that no child should have to deal with. There was clearly no other adult there to step in and take responsibility, so all his energy and emotions were spent on taking care of his grandmother when they should have been spent on schoolwork, extracurricular activities, and other adolescent concerns.

I believe that many children who suffer from anger problems do so mostly because of an unstable home. This is why many of them are placed on medication to help control their anger and mood swings. Children who are identified as having an anger problem must be taught how to exercise self-restraint when it comes to controlling their anger.

I believe it would be much more economical and smarter if we, as parents and leaders, took the time to begin building our children the right way in their younger years, the *first* time around. When physical buildings are too dangerous to reside in, or when their structures are too unstable to remain standing, they are unfit and are either torn down or major remodeling work must be undertaken. Sometimes, we say that they are "condemned." Likewise, when we leave children to deal with their anger problems alone, we are condemning them in some ways: we deny them the chance to live a productive and anger-free life. It's not that they become unfit to live, but in many cases, they don't know *how* to live, or they may find that no one else wants to live around them. They will spiritually, emotionally, and physically fall apart. When this happens, they will require our help in some form or another anyway. So, parents have a choice: they can spend the time while their children are young, or they can spend a lifetime trying to rehabilitate and support their children when they are older. Anger just gets angrier.

Be Aware of Timed-Released Anger

Many people deal with their anger problems in a more conservative way. Often, they hold their frustrations and displeasure with life within themselves, at least, until they cannot contain them any longer. Some people manage to repress years of anger, until one day they have a major breakdown and lose control. Their anger may have been building day after day, week after week, month after month, year after year, for a very long time. One day, something unfavorable—whether major or minor—takes place in their life, and they explode from the inside out.

I have seen this happen with adolescents and teens who have had their childhood taken away from them, especially among those who were physically or sexually abused, or bullied, or among those who happen to look, act, or dress differently. We also see this type of anger in children who grow up in single-parent homes, in homes with two parents present where there is little or no positive relationship, and in homes where some form of domestic violence has been taking place.

Certain children are prone to timed-released anger, in particular those who experienced some type of emotional or sociological trauma in their younger years, those who were forced to grow up too soon or who had to provide for themselves or the rest of the family, and those who were forced to maintain their own safety and care, because no parent or guardian was available to do this for them. This type of anger is especially common among adolescents and teenage boys whose fathers are not in their lives. Timed-released anger is also common among children who are picked on and bullied by others to the point that they feel helpless and unheard.

Timed-released anger can be illustrated by imagining a balloon slowly being filled with too much air. The wall of the balloon gets thinner and thinner as the balloon gets bigger—until there is no more room for any more air, and it explodes. It is not the outside of the balloon that weakens, but the inside. Likewise, children that conserve their angry outbursts for long periods will weaken from within, causing major, outwardly visible behaviors later.

Timed-released anger can also be viewed as what is known as a "ticking time bomb." You know there will be an explosion, but you don't know exactly when and where it will happen. Bomb squads work fast to disarm a bomb that has been set; they don't wait for it to self-destruct and then focus on the damage caused by the explosion. Those of us in positions of authority—parents, leaders, or otherwise—can't wait until the anger within a child causes them to self-destruct, damaging their lives and the lives of those around them. Yet this is what we see happening in our society more and more. Afterward, those who thought they knew the person will say that he or she was always "polite, kind, and didn't bother anyone." Their friends and acquaintances will say, "I never thought they would do something like this." Seldom is there any remorse, apologies, or sorrow expressed for their actions.

We see this type of action in people who are grown and who appear to be living a normal, productive life. Something traumatic or horrific will happen in their life to cause them to go into a state of depression, and afterward, they never let themselves outwardly express their feelings. It could be the death of a child, a close family member, or a close friend, or it could be a divorce, a failed relationship, or the loss of a job. These people, although they seem to be doing fine on the exterior, have chosen to live with internal anger. This anger brewing within will eventually find its way out, causing the person to do or act in such an explosive or unusual way that it surprises even themselves.

Timed-released anger can cause a person to do things or to conduct themselves in ways that they never would have considered previously. This is why I believe it's important to teach children how to talk and outwardly express their emotions and feelings when they are young, especially after something horrific or traumatic has happened in their lives. If their anger is left to take care of itself, it will rear its ugly head one day in the future, and the sight might not be pretty.

When children are left to destruct, much damage is done. The many horrific crimes we witness people committing, such as child or spousal abuse, are not because of situations that develop overnight or over the course of a few weeks. They are events that result from the buildup of anger over a long period of time without any intervention. We must find a way to do a better job of identifying when children are conserving or repressing their anger. If we wait for the explosion to happen, we might be in the area of destruction.

I encourage teens to seek help quickly if they find themselves hording this type of anger. I challenge parents to get help for their children if they suspect any emotional or psychological trauma or anxiety of any kind. These feelings will not get any better when they are ignored, but will almost certainly get worse with time.

Avoid Negative Influences

Negative influences will always cause friction between what one is taught as being right and wrong. Negative influences have a way of taking over one's desire and will for life. If someone or something causes friction between what one feels or thinks, and what one is hearing or doing, stop and check oneself. Someone once said, "Misery loves company." I have found that a person who loves having a pity party for oneself always likes to invite company. They have this attitude about themselves that says, "Nothing is going right for me, and therefore, I am going to invite someone else to experience what I am experiencing by sending out negative influences."

Negative influences are destructive to one's way of living. They will create thoughts and ideas in the mind that one would never imagine. Negative influences will cause one to go places and get involved in activities that will destroy the dreams and visions one once had for his or her life. Teens who allow negative influences to invade and control their minds are being ruled and jerked around like puppets on a string. The negative influences tell them how they should act, talk, dress, and where to go. Teens are sometimes hit so hard and so fast with these negative influences that to reject them would seem unrealistic and unsocial.

I have learned in my many years of living that the one person who has control over any kind of influence on me is me alone. I have discovered that I am in control of my actions. It's up to me what I allow or disallow to control my emotions. Negative influences can come by many means, but they normally come by way of people. These people can be considered friends, family, or acquaintances. Negative influences can also be brought on by environmental elements. But just because negative influences show up in one's environment doesn't mean that he or she must allow them to change his or her beliefs and teachings. I can't stop people from saying negative things and doing negative things to me, but I do have the ability to control how I react to them. I believe it is better to teach children at a young age that people are going to say and do things that they will not appreciate and agree with.

When it comes to adolescents, I think negative influences are one of the driving forces behind most of their negative behaviors. Many times, the young people who go off into drama do so because of negative influences. Many of them get so involved and engaged in the drama that they lose all train of thought. I have talked to several teens that have reached this level and come to understand that most of them never meant to go there and didn't intend to take it that far. So, what happened? Why weren't they able to resist the negative influences? This is the power that negative influences have on a person. Negative influences, when allowed to control one's behavior, are like an addiction. People that are addicted to some sort of substance find themselves wanting that substance, and eventually, it controls how they live. Likewise, negative influences will become a magnet-like substance and intrude on a major part of their life.

In my experience in dealing with teens, negative influences are a major cause for so many of them going down a path that neither they nor their parents had planned on. I have witnessed firsthand how teens are controlled and led by negative influences. At times, it seems as though all their energy is absorbed by these negative influences, and this drives them to participate in certain activities or conduct themselves with such bad behaviors that it affects their whole day. Sometimes, this goes on for weeks or months at a time.

Earlier, I spoke of the friction that is caused by what one knows to be right and what one is being told is right (even when it's wrong). Placing a positively charged battery cable on a negative battery post will result in a spark 100% of the time. The two cannot stand to meet each other without creating a spark. When a child is taught to do the right thing and be respectful both in words and in deeds, they will recognize, and with every effort, try to reject negative influences that try to invade their personal space. The tension that they will feel gives them the opportunity to pull away. Negative influences must be off-limits. Negative influences result in negative behavior. Negative behaviors result in a negative lifestyle. A negative lifestyle results in a negative future.

One Sunday morning in church, the mother of a teenage girl walked over to where my wife and I were sitting and shared her heart with me. She began to tell me how her sixteen-year-old daughter had left home and that she had not been seen or heard from. This mother was in tears and frightened for her daughter. She went on to tell me how she had already been to the police station to file a missing person's report as well as a juvenile runaway petition for her daughter's return. She confessed that this was the first time the girl had ever left home. Then she said the words I had been expecting all along: "She's been hanging out with this girl I don't trust who is involved in drugs and other negative behaviors." That was it. That was the underlying cause of her daughter leaving home: negative influences that caused her to refuse to obey authority in her home. The influence of her friend had more power over her than the authoritative methods of her mother. The father of this sixteen-year-old girl was never mentioned. I concluded that the father had no influence on his daughter's life, or at least, no positive influence. Influence is powerful, whether it is negative or positive.

There were many times as a teenager when I too went against the authority of my parents, but every time I did so, I ended up regretting it. I have a message for all young people out there: "Don't embrace the influence of people in your age group." Why would you think they know better than your parents or other adults? If for some reason you just can't accept what your parents tell you, then take action to find someone you can trust, and then seek advice from them. A good place to start is a teacher, school counselor, or another family member. The main concern is that you get help.

This takes me back to the question of whom or what is teaching our children. If our children are being taught to recognize and avoid negative influences, they will have the opportunity to live a more successful life. Children that are taught to avoid negative influences will always be one step ahead of those who are driven and led by negative influences. These students will have a positive influence on others and on their own future. My challenge to you is to use your positive influence to help change another young person. Negative influential people love to be around negative influential people. Positive influential people love to be around positive influential people. What type are you being influenced by?

Learn How to Deal with Life Interruptions

As we face life, you and I will be challenged with things that will interfere with our daily lives. We must all learn to somehow get past them and go on with life. As you may have guessed by now, life is not perfect, and we all have things in our lives that affect each of us in different ways. For you and me to avoid a personal meltdown and possibly fall into a crisis, it's vital that each one of us takes personal responsibility to deal with the uncertainty.

We all have heard the saying, "An ounce of prevention is worth a pound of cure." I believe in taking preventative measures to try to stop something from happening. Granted, you and I can't predict what's going to happen tomorrow, and no one can predict when life interruptions will invade his or her daily life. I learned early in my life that most of the time, things wouldn't always turn out to be the way I envisioned them, and that there would be unwelcome circumstances that would interrupt my normal, daily life.

I have the military to thank for teaching me about life interruptions. In the military, I always experienced things that would come and change the plans of the day. There was no need to stress or get a negative attitude about changes and delays in my scheduled plans. I had to learn to deal with it. The phrase, "hurry up and wait" is known throughout the military. We were always told something like, "The mission has changed or taken on a new goal." Because of this, it better prepared me for not only a career in the military but also for life after the military.

It was very shocking to learn and acknowledge in my thirties that life was not fair and was not even close to being perfect. I prefer to teach prevention than to do intervention. It saddens me to watch teens and adolescents lose all moral character when their daily living is altered because of life's interruptions. In my experience working with middle and high school students, interventions were mostly needed simply because of interruptions. Many times, the person brought the interruptions upon themselves. I understand that there are cases when certain interruptions, such as those that cause physical or emotional distress, may warrant professional intervention. But many times, the interruptions that teens experience are not life-changing at all. They do not have a permanent effect on their lives, and most of the time, the results are only temporary. In all cases, one must learn to deal with them when they happen.

When we plan on one thing and something totally different happens, it's not the time to give up on life. Plans are just what they are—plans. Plans are subject to change without any prior notice or input from one's opinion. If all plans were played out just as we scheduled or imagined them, you and I would have boring lives. When we have a plan that fails to go the way we intended it, I believe it causes one to adjust and make corrections for future planning. It is also an opportunity to learn and grow in life. The goal of planning is not to have everything perfect in our lives, because it never will be, but planning gives us a sense of pleasure and completeness. For instance, whenever my wife and I are planning to travel somewhere, I feel much better when I can sit down and figure out the distance we must drive, the best route to take, and the approximate amount of money we will need for gas. Yes, I can take the trip without doing all these things, but when I do them during my planning stage, I can better accept and deal with unexpected mishaps that may occur along the way.

I believe many people have failed to walk in their destiny because they were driven off course by distractions and interruptions in life. If they had been warned about these things and taught how to deal with them, they likely would have had a better chance at finding success.

Because life is already short, I believe it's important that young people be informed about unexpected interruptions in their lives and how important it is that they learn how to deal with them in order to avoid a self-induced crisis. If one can learn to look for some good in all life interruptions, the bad won't stand out so much, and life will be more fulfilling.

Chapter Three
Decide What You Want Out of Life

Nothing saddens me more than watching young people go through life without a clue of where they are headed or would like to end up. Granted, no one has all the answers and, therefore, probably won't ever know his or her destination in this life. But I think it's important for young people, especially teens, to have some sort of landmark to aim for.

Lawrence J. Peters, a United States educator and writer, was on to something when he penned these words: "If you don't know where you are going, you will probably end up somewhere else." I have witnessed these words play out in so many people's lives. They never seem to get a snapshot of what they want out of life. People who think they can live life without vision and focus are living in a state of deception. Our life will happen without us getting involved in it, but it won't happen in nearly the way we thought it would happen. A person's life is bound to take on the events that society dictates. Moreover, if one plans nothing, nothing will happen; at least, nothing that will be productive and worth getting excited about.

People who earned success through the labor of their own hands and hard work didn't just live each day as if a successful life was automatically going to happen for them. At some point, they decided what it was they wanted out of life. They probably didn't know all the details of what it would take to get there, but they had a snapshot of what they wanted their life to be like.

I believe that the younger a person is when they decide what they want out of life, the more realistic the chances are of achieving it. In my own life, I have learned that the earlier I started to focus on my future, the greater the chance I had of seeing those things come to pass. Teens are at the age where they can imagine things that can be accomplished with focus and hard work. Imagine what your life would be like if you had an attainable goal set in your mind. It was Albert Einstein who said, "Your imagination is your preview of life's coming attractions."

At some point in time, we all have images in our minds of how we would like to see our lives played out. Granted, some people wait way too late in life to form these images in their minds. Will everything you imagine, or the way you imagine it, happen exactly that way? No! But I discovered in my own life that every time I got a passion for something and then decided to explore it, the imagination of it started to happen. Imagination about your life and future is not something that will happen automatically. One must decide that he or she wants to live a successful, fruitful life. Imagination is a byproduct of decision-making. Once a person has decided what they want out of life, they start to imagine what it will look like and what it might take to get there.

It is without question that many teens lose out on a major part of their developing years by not imagining what their future could be like. When the human mind is left to wander on its own, most of the time, it places images in the mind that give a picture of where that person is, what they are going through, how bad it is, how bad it might get, and how things might not get any better. If these are images that you don't want to float around in your mind, the only way to change them is to first decide you want a better life and future for yourself and then decide on what steps you need to take to get there. Your mind will begin to wander in that direction. As your mind wanders in that direction, you will begin to speak words related to those things, which will form images in your mind.

I believe that every successful person asked him or herself at some point in life what he or she wanted out of it, or at least thought about it. Dreams and visions only come to pass after one has imagined them, and then acted on them.

Life Happens

Life is like vapor. You take a few steps off into it, look around, and it's gone. Having a glimpse of where you want to go in life is important, as we discussed earlier, but the journey one travels on the way is just as important, if not more. Too much focus on one's destination while overlooking one's path on that journey could cost one success. Everyday life is a journey. You and I are heading somewhere from where we are right at this moment. Along the way, there are resources and people to assist and help us get where we are going. Though the destination is important, if we focus too deeply on it, we will miss the blessings that were placed along the way to help guide us on our journey to our destination.

Our life is going to happen, regardless of what we choose to do. This is not something you or I have control over. But what we do have control over is how we choose to *live* it. Just as a news reporter will always have news to report, we will always experience life happening to us and around us. A news reporter can select what to report and choose how to report it, whether it's good or bad, exciting or sad—it is a choice they make. Likewise, our life will always be in the "happening" mode. But how we live is a choice we make.

Because life happens so fast, I believe that it's important that adolescents remain attached to their lifeline—that is, their parents—all through their developing years. Too many times, I have witnessed young people leaving home simply because they chose not to be under supervision or authority. Many young people have the desire to leave home while they are still teenagers. What they fail to realize is that they are about to enter a world that will also put them under its supervision and authority, and this type of supervision and authority has many voices that they will be required to answer to. When a child leaves their parents before the appropriate time, it is like picking fruit from its vine before it is fully ripe. If children stay under the care, supervision, and authority of their parents, they will be better equipped to face the adult life ahead of them. Children of the same age don't grow up faster than others, some just mature faster. The more mature they are, the more responsibility can be granted. Maturity does not mean that they are grown up and ready for life.

Too often, many people zoom in so close on what they want their future to look like, that the path to take them there becomes blurry. This is caused by placing more focus on the future than on what is presently at hand. On the journey is where one will discover the directions, corrections, and instructions necessary to reach our destination. These elements are important because they assist us in staying on the right path, which aids in the completion of our goal. Life is lived one day at a time. This is not to say that planning and vision are not important. Someone said, "Fail to plan, plan to fail." But face it, we cannot live life on Monday, skip Tuesday, Wednesday, and Thursday, and then jump right into Friday. Each day in between must be lived to arrive at Friday, which is the destination for many working people. I hear people say all the time on Monday, "If I can just make it to Friday." What they really mean is that they have four days before Friday, and they realize that the days between Monday and Friday must be lived out. This is how life happens. There are no shortcuts, life *will* happen.

It would be wise for teens to acknowledge and utilize all the resources and people placed along the way on their journey to help them achieve success. Wouldn't it be great if they lived in such a way that focusing on their journey through life was a prerequisite to their destination? I believe many young people are in such a hurry to grow up that they overlook all the important elements on their journey, which are necessary to help them develop into mature, successful people. Each day, there are new ideals and visions along each young person's journey that are essential to their destination. Moving too fast and having tunnel vision on the outcome or the destination means that we can miss all the little golden nuggets along the way.

Life happens regardless of our troubles and problems. If we have plans for a long life and a successful future, we cannot avoid our journey. The best thing to do is make the journey an exciting and enjoyable one by "sightseeing" along the way. We just might discover some interesting things worth gathering. When you spray an air freshener in your home or car, you will see a mist, and then suddenly, it disappears. But the smell stays there for some time. Likewise, your life and my life are the same. Our lives happen just that fast, but what we do along the way, whether good or bad, will linger a while and could prove to be negative or positive.

Someone said, "Life is ten percent what happens to you and ninety percent how you respond to it." Negative and bad things are going to happen in our lives. But the real challenge is how we respond to them. Your life is happening right now, wherever you are and whatever you are doing. It's not how you start, but how you finish. Finish strong!

Living Life on Autopilot Won't Work

I have often wondered how much better and more convenient the journey of life would be if there were no bumps and curves on the path. Imagine, one day you are born and from that day forward, your life goes in the direction you want it to. Wake up! You are dreaming.

Life cannot be lived on autopilot, and no one can simply expect to achieve whatever they want living that way. On your journey through life, there are bumps and curves that will require you to make corrections to get back on course. There are turns, stops, and slowdowns, and you must use your knowledge and experience to decide what is best for the next step in your life's journey.

Wouldn't it be wonderful if we could somehow set our cars on autopilot so they would take us wherever we wanted to go without any other actions from us? What if we could start driving, and after we got on the interstate, we could simply relax and take our hands off the steering wheel? I know there are automobiles built to perform this task, but I wouldn't totally rely on it. Your car might drive between the lines for a short distance, but eventually, it starts to veer off to the right or left. Without physically correcting the steering wheel, your car will end up off the road. Likewise, in our daily lives, we will experience bumps, curves, stops, and turns, and we will need to make corrections. If we are negligent in making the necessary corrections to get our lives back on track, we will be forced off our path.

Even a pilot who has put his plane on autopilot must at some point adjust in order to arrive at the desired destination. If he leaves the plane on autopilot from the time he leaves the ground to the time he lands, he will get off course. I believe we as parents and leaders have left many of our children to live life on autopilot. We have left them to find their own way when many of them don't have a clue where they are or where they are going in life.

It is vital that parents make themselves available and get involved in their children's lives instead of just leaving them on autopilot. Adolescents and teens must be steered and redirected when they drift off course. It is not a matter of *whether* they go off course, but *when* they get off course. Parents must be there to help their children make the necessary adjustments, tweaks, and changes to help them get back on course. As children, they will experience the bumps, curves, stops, and turns in life. When we as parents and leaders allow our children to go through life on autopilot, they are sure to crash at some point. And when this happens, we must then spend our time and money trying to repair them and get them fit for life again.

Unfortunately, however, many times the crash "totals" the adolescent's life, and the damage is irreparable. Parents, leaders, and all those in positions of authority must take every opportunity and make every effort to ensure our children don't go through life on autopilot. This is my sole purpose for writing this book. We must save our children.

Don't Take Offense to "No" Answers

Previously, I told you about the first grader who didn't like to be told "no." Most of us dislike hearing the word "no" too, as it relates to what we want and how we think certain things should be. But to tell you the truth, in many situations, "no" isn't such a bad or negative word. Why do many of us often view the word "no" as a negative or bad word? Let me be the first to admit that there have been times when I received a "no" answer, which altered my whole life. Like the time I was told "no" by the Army about my military retirement request; it had not been approved. Or the time when I was told "no," I didn't get the position or the job I had applied for. But these were not a permanent "no," they were just a "not yet," because it wasn't the right time for the things I was trying to do.

Oftentimes, "no" is taken as an offense, but it is sometimes the best answer we need. It may not be what we expected or wanted to hear, but it really can work in our favor. Many times, when people seek information or clarification about a situation, or ask for permission, when they hear the answer "no," they get offended. Why? He or she got the information they were seeking. Why wasn't "no" an acceptable answer? Not only is it viewed as unacceptable, but also, they take offense at it. Why? He or she got their answer but became offended because it was not the answer they wanted to hear.

I remember growing up as a child, and most of the time, the word "no" did not register with me. Whenever I couldn't get my way or get what I wanted and was told "no," I took offense and immediately developed a bad attitude toward the person it came from. Most of the time, this "no" came out of the mouth of my mother or father. I was too young and immature to understand that my father and mother were telling me "no," because they had my best interests at heart. I didn't understand that they held the wisdom and knowledge to know what was best for me. I believe that most of the "no" answers came from their experiences of living life. Sometimes, personal experience is the best teaching tool a parent can offer his or her child. My father passed away at 95 years old, but I was still gaining wisdom from him up until the day he passed, just by having father-to-son conversations.

Turn Your Negative "No" Into a Positive "Yes"

Teens, hear me well: the next time your father or mother drops the "no" word on you, don't take offense, but instead, try to see things from their point of view. Remind yourself that your parents love you and they provide for you. Remember how hard they have worked to bring you to the point in life where you are. Get an attitude of thanksgiving about the fact that your parents chose to give you a chance at life and not abort you. Life is a gift from God, but your parents had the opportunity to deny you that gift, and instead, they chose life for you.

Before you allow yourself to get offended and develop a negative attitude at the word "no" from your parents, take a few seconds to think about why they may have said "no" in that circumstance. Remember, it doesn't have to be permanent, it just may not be timely. Most parents, I believe, are willing to explain to their children why they told them no. When this happens, it is an excellent opportunity for you, the child, to take the negative "no" and turn it into a positive "yes." Parents have a reason for their choices, and most of the time, the child doesn't have a clue about the danger they could have been exposed to if some other choice was granted. This is a good opportunity for teens and adolescents to use their imagination. They can imagine reasons or situations as to why their parents told them "no" and come to an understanding within themselves, so that they can respond, "Yes, I think I understand." If each child would make this process a part of his or her life, then when the "no" comes, they will know how to get past it and move forward.

Remember the first grader who had meltdowns when he was told "no." Just think for a moment. If this child was allowed to continue through life with such negative feelings about the word "no," he would be bound to live a self-destructive life. Corrections were vital to get and keep him on the right course.

As I have observed teens' negative behavior over the years, it is an understatement to say that many of them get pretty angry when they are told "no." I don't think I acted in such a way when I was this age, or at least, I don't remember doing so. But if I did, it was only a few times, because my parents would certainly make sure I had something to get angry about. But the society we live in today has a major effect on teens and adolescents when it comes to them having their way about certain things. Some adolescents refuse to accept "no" for an answer. They fail to consider the long-term negative effects it could have on their life, their parents, and all the people around them.

This is a major problem in our public schools today. Some students turn into another person when they hear the word "no." They are so focused on the current pleasure of the moment and so short-sighted that nothing less than a "yes" will please them. Pleasure is not the goal here. The goal is to try to understand why your parents, teachers, administrators, and all the people in authority chose the answer they did. It was not to deny anyone's rights. While working as a school security officer, I was reminded of this daily. Really, the only right a student has in a public school environment is the right to an education. Everything else they are allowed is a privilege. What they fail to understand is that privileges are subject to withdrawal.

Many teens also believe that they are entitled to certain privileges in school, and they feel they should be in control of what they are or are not allowed to do. This is far from the truth. The only things that a child is entitled to in a school setting are a safe learning environment and a fair chance to receive an education. From my point of view, the only things children are really in control of are their personal actions and their attitudes. Everything else is subject to authority. I have witnessed many students lose these entitlements simply because they did not know how to deal with and respond to a "no" answer.

There is a saying that I was taught in the military that has stuck with me all these years, "Abuse it, lose it." When one is granted the privilege to participate in a certain activity or go to a particular place, it is his or her responsibility to maintain order so that the person who approved and granted the privilege has no reason to revoke it.

Body Language Speaks Volumes

A person's body language will tell what they are really thinking and feeling regardless of what they outwardly express. Many times, a person doesn't even have to say a word regarding an issue before one can figure out where they stand on it. Just observe their body language, and you will instantly get a general feeling of what they really feel and think. People can tell you one thing, but their body language will reveal the truth. A person's body language can even determine his or her future in life. Body language that shows someone possesses a positive attitude, even when problems arise, will often result in a more positive outcome. Body language that reveals the person possesses a negative attitude will many times result in a negative outcome.

I taught myself that when I was called in to deal with a student because of some behavior problem, the first thing to do was observe their body language. This helped me determine what the child is feeling and how they may react to increased authority. It has also prevented me and others in my care from getting hurt. If the situation allows it, I will try to make sure my approach toward the child presents me as a person who is cool, calm, and in control. It is important that my body language be as positive as possible. I have found that an emotional and distrusting child exhibiting negative body language needs to witness the body language of those in authority as being confident and in control. Negative body language in an already negative situation will only make things more complicated. But as important as it is for those in authority to possess positive body language, it is equally as important for children to possess positive body language at home, in their community, and at school.

Be Responsible for Your Actions

Personal responsibility is not a popular thing with many people today. This is even hard for some grown people to do, not just teenagers. It is common for some people to act a certain way or do certain things but never be willing to take personal responsibility for their actions. This is why children must be taught the importance of being responsible for their actions, whether good or bad, while they are young. Children must be taught that life is not perfect, and neither are they. Teaching children that they will make mistakes and make some poor choices in their lives is vital for the health and well-being of every child. It is easy to claim responsibility when one's actions are seen as good and are intended for a noble cause. But when one's actions turn out to be bad and unfavorable in the eyes of others, it is not as easy to claim responsibility for them. I have witnessed many children get angry at others when *they* are caught in acts of poor choices. They will fault everyone but themselves. What they are angry about is the fact that they were caught; there is little or no sorrow for what they did.

I don't believe that there is one parent who would like to see their child get into any kind of trouble. Many times, children are taught to lie about a situation or just remain silent. Both could get one into more trouble than just simply telling the truth. I have learned that it is better to tell the truth at the first opportunity. Telling a lie will only lead to telling another lie! From there, everything snowballs if the truth is not told. Lying about one's action is like spreading molasses in a chair, sitting in it, and expecting not to get sticky. Not owning up to one's actions will put a person in a sticky situation. It is much better to start out by accepting personal responsibility for our actions.

Accepting personal responsibility up front will result in two things. First, it will give you a feeling of peace that you did the right thing. Secondly, your credibility will remain intact with those who believe in you. You can gain the respect of others by making your words a bond to those who hear them. That means you say what you mean and mean what you say; you keep your word and are trustworthy. It is never too late to take personal responsibility for our actions if the opportunity is still available. We can always decide to tell the truth, but we don't always do so.

Some will argue that personal responsibility comes with the age of accountability. I am not trying to start a debate, but at what age is a person considered accountable? Is it during the teens? After witnessing the behaviors and actions of many adolescents, I have come to believe that a person can be held accountable for their actions at different ages. I think that there is an age when each child begins to learn and understand what is right and what is wrong. I believe that this stems from their environment and the things that each individual child is exposed to. I would argue that when they begin to learn and understand right from wrong, that is when their "age of accountability" begins.

Some children know that lying is a bad thing. Either they have been taught this, or they have learned it through experience. If people continue to involve themselves in actions that result in destructive outcomes, they will learn that doing the same thing repeatedly will get the same result: destruction. If children grow up in a home where they are exposed to drugs and alcohol, and if they witness time and time again someone getting arrested, or even worse, dying from the drugs and alcohol, then the child is most likely going to learn at an earlier age about the danger that drug and alcohol abuse can bring. Unfortunately, these same behavior patterns are oftentimes carried out by the children who witness them, despite already knowing and understanding the consequences of those decisions.

Today, we live in a society where children are exposed to things that 20 or 30 years ago, they would not have been exposed to. It is important that adolescents admit when they have done wrong. This is especially important in school settings. Teachers and administrators should not have to try and figure out who is telling the truth when there are incidents in school. Remember, telling the truth and accepting responsibility for your actions, says a lot about your character as a person. It shows that you are responsible and willing to admit when you have made a mistake or crossed over into an area where you were not allowed.

Sometimes, we will be asked to tell the truth about another person. Many times, people are unwilling to cooperate when it comes to giving out information about someone they know and like. In school settings, the students view sharing of information as "snitching." Most children will not snitch on each other. They see this as a form of being disloyal, even if that person is in danger or is causing destruction to themself or others. When one chooses to withhold information for whatever reason, it takes away the opportunity for the other person to be responsible for their actions.

Granted, there are many times when one should not get involved in another's affairs. But if withholding information will in any way put you, your classmates, your family, or your school in danger, then snitching is recommended. By snitching on a friend or someone in your peer group, you are actually helping them by allowing them to tell the truth from their own mouth. If they truly love and care about their friends, snitching could be the best thing to do when the information is important. Snitching could save a life. Be responsible and tell the truth. Don't wait for someone to tell you that you are wrong when you already know you are. Be responsible and be the first to acknowledge that you are wrong, then work to make it right, if possible.

Being responsible for your actions also means being responsible for the consequences of your actions. Even if your actions are the result of a mistake, poor judgment, or a lack of knowledge on your part, you must be willing to take full responsibility for the consequences of your actions. Many times, people fail to accept the punishment for their actions. We sometimes look for others to receive part or all of the punishment, but accepting responsibility for your actions will help you grow mentally and become more mature. No one else is going to jail for you if you get caught stealing. Your parents will not be the ones who get locked up if you drink and drive. Your parents or your best friends won't be the ones suspended from school if you get caught violating school board policies. *You* commit the action, *you* accept the consequences for it. It's just that simple.

What police officer would stop a person for speeding and then write the speeding ticket to someone else? What teacher would take another student to the administrator's office because of someone else's negative behavior in the classroom? In most cases, the law does not require parents to be criminally charged in place of their children when the child commits an offense, nor would you expect to be put on trial for something someone else was accused of doing. In the same way, you shouldn't expect someone else to weather the storm for your bad and negative behavior.

Some children choose to make wrong or bad choices even after they have been properly taught by their parents. I know there are many parents who are successful at teaching their children right from wrong and good from evil. As I said before, most parents try hard to teach their children good morals, but let's be realistic. Children don't always do and say what they are taught to do and say by their parents. Children must understand that the consequences they face from their negative behaviors will not be paid for by someone else, not even their parents. It comes down to personal responsibility.

Children won't always be around their parents or an authority figure. This is the time when their real character is shown—when their *free will* is at play. When the choice is made to involve oneself in a negative behavior, one must be willing to accept any consequences that come as a result of that. If you were taught the rights and wrongs of life at an early age, and yet you made the choice to go against all you know and did something to get in trouble, guess what? *You* pay the consequences. All that your parents and friends can do is stand back and watch. Yes, your parents will support you in the process, and rightly so, but you have to suffer the consequences, and your parents get to worry.

Many children will do and say what their friends or others in their environment do or say. Many children will follow the patterns of those in their age group, even though they understand them to be wrong and not approved by their parents. Adolescents and teens listen with both ears; you can come from one of the best homes, with both parents present, and you can be taught all the moral values and godly principles as a small child, but if you make the choice to involve yourself in negative actions and behaviors, you get to suffer the consequences. My advice is to stick to the teachings and instructions you received from your parents or other trusted authority figures.

I remember when I was preparing to involve myself in some sort of negative behavior as a teenager, I would always get this feeling that what I was about to do or where I was about to go was *wrong*. I knew that my parents would not approve of it. What my parents taught me at home went with me everywhere I went. At this point, I had the *free will* to choose to either continue with the negative behavior or change direction. The time will come when we all must grow up, take personal responsibility for our actions, and be willing to face the consequences. Parents have the responsibility of teaching their children right from wrong, but children have the responsibility of choosing to obey those teachings, even when the parents are nowhere around. If you choose otherwise, be prepared to take responsibility and accept the consequences.

Guilty by Association

Every person's character will be judged by the company they keep. It's no different for adolescents. Who you associate with will label you as being good or bad. Children love to hang out with others their age, but I have a word of warning—be careful about the company you keep! Association is a powerful force controlling many children today. Many adolescents find themselves running with the wrong crowd or going to the wrong places. Whether or not they have an official part in the plans or actions of a particular group, if they are associated with that group in any way, there is guilt by association. Others will assume that they were involved in whatever transpires by choice. Young people must understand and acknowledge that they do not have to physically participate in an activity to be labeled as willing participants. All it takes is association with that person or group.

When a person associates with a group or cause, they are viewed by others as being an active part of that group or cause. A person might not truly believe in the actions of someone else, but if they are discovered to be an associate of that person, then they are looked at as having the same beliefs and sharing in the same activities, whether good or bad. In most cases, the "innocent until proven guilty" reverts to "guilty until proven innocent." While that may not seem fair, it is just reality. If you don't want to be labeled as a troublemaker, you should avoid hanging out with known troublemakers. If you don't want to be labeled as a gangbanger, then you should avoid hanging out with and dressing like gangbangers.

Young people must be taught that there are places they should not go and people they should not seek fellowship with. The earlier children begin learning this, the sooner they will begin to realize that it is not a good thing to show up at certain places and hang out with certain people. There are many people, young and old, that are serving time behind bars because they were found guilty by the court for simply being a victim of association. There are many people, young and old, whose life was cut short simply because they were associated with people that were out looking for trouble and by that association, were found to be guilty as well.

I have had some close calls in my lifetime simply because I was with a group of people or in a certain place when a crime was committed. Even though I had no knowledge that a crime was going to take place, I did have knowledge that the people I was hanging out with were labeled as troublemakers. The places that I chose to go and hang out were places that had a history of trouble, where law enforcement personnel were always present. I put myself in some dangerous situations as a teen. The point I am trying to get across is this: there are some places that teens do not need to be associated with by going there, and there are some people they do not need to be associated with by hanging out with them.

Even if you were taught how to behave in public and around others, there is a saying that is true 100% of the time: "Bad company corrupts good character."

Chapter Four
A Treasure Waiting to be Discovered

I believe that deep down inside of every human being there is an undiscovered treasure waiting to be found. You and I may not know it even existed unless we explored and started to dig to remove those things that we don't like about ourselves. To change for the good, once we discover all the negative and unproductive things in our lives, we must seek to find that which is positive and good within us. The discovery process can be a painful one if we have spent years of living as though it counts for nothing. The discovery process starts when we are willing to lay aside the old ways of doing things and begin a journey of exploration of the inner self. This is when we begin to discover a treasure within that will change our lives for the better.

What you and I look at on the outside should not be the complete picture we have of ourselves. Your potential is found in your ability to believe that there is greatness on the inside. To discover that greatness, you must start the process of peeling off layers of unwanted and nonproductive activities. In my own life, I have had layers of unwanted stuff clinging and attaching to me—stuff that I didn't ask for. Because of good godly teaching from my parents, I knew that I couldn't sit back and allow this so-called "stuff" to define who I was and what I would become in life. At some point, I had to take control and tell myself, "This is not who I am, nor what I want to become."

Take an onion, for example. If you look at the outer portion, it doesn't look too appealing to the eyes, but after you begin to peel away the outer layers, you discover that the layers underneath are more appetizing. Likewise, your life is like an onion. As we go through life and face challenges, setbacks, and disappointments, layers of unwanted stuff can begin to accumulate upon us. We must be willing to peel away the parts that we don't like about ourselves. We must look deep into our souls and realize the treasure that lies deep within. The peeling must take place first, and it starts in one's mind.

Consider a miner. Miners must dig deep into the ground to discover the most expensive and precious stones. Through training and experience, the miner has learned that the best materials a mine has to offer are not found on the surface, but deep within, underneath layers of dirt and rock. He must diligently work to dig and remove the things that have no value to him and don't achieve his purpose. Likewise, you and I will never experience the greatness that we are capable of until we look past what's on the outside and begin to visualize the potential that lies deep within us. Pulling out the greatness in you will start with a change in your mental attitude. Your mental attitude will make all the difference in whether you are able to discover the hidden treasures buried deep within your soul. Having the right mental attitude about things that you face in life will determine whether you will live as a productive contributor to society.

Parents are responsible for making sure their children have what it takes for them to function and survive in this world. Parents take extra care to ensure their infant is fed the right formula, with the recommendations of their doctor, to make sure that the baby receives the right nutrients in the right balance. Such care shouldn't stop when children reach the adolescent years. The adolescent years are just as important as the infant years when it comes to providing a child with what they need to survive. No parent wants their child to become malnourished, whether in their infant stage or adolescent stage. Just like a child must be given the right foods in their infancy to properly grow and mature in their physical body, likewise, adolescents need the training, stability, and structure to live a well-balanced and productive life.

Get Your Mind Right Before You Start to Dig

I learned about the importance of having a positive mental attitude while serving in the military. Daily physical training exercises were something I enjoyed. Rising early every morning and running for four or five miles was a breeze. Doing push-ups and sit-ups was just a part of my daily routine and came easy to me as well. But whenever it was time for my bi-yearly physical fitness test, I could feel the anxiety building. Just the thought of the word "test" would send negative thoughts running through my mind. I would feel the pressure starting to take control of my mind.

In my mind was where I had to overcome the thought of failing or injuring myself during the test. I was in good physical condition and knew that my physical body would have no problem performing. My body was capable, but my mind was trying to tell me something different. Each time, I had to tell myself that I was in good physical condition, and that I would breeze through my physical fitness test. I had to pull out the greatness inside me by making myself remember how I loved to run and do exercises. I had to remind myself of all the previous tests I had passed with no problems. The inner strength was always there, I just had to dig for it—after I decided that I wasn't going to allow my mind to control and dictate my actions, which inevitably would have had a negative effect on my performance.

I was having a conversation with a young man who was a football coach at a local high school. We started to talk about the physical build of some male high school teens. He was saying that some of the players he coached have the physical bodies it takes to play football, but for some reason just could not perform at game time. He then started to tell me that he would tell each one of them to first decide in his mind that he would produce success on the field during the game. He said he always reminded them that each of them had to say what it was they wanted to accomplish. He communicated to each player that it was important that they hear themselves say what they wanted to gain during the game. This coach knew the importance of pulling out the greatness in each player and knew it would help them find the ability to do great things on the field.

He was teaching his players about the importance of having a positive mental mindset despite what each of them might be feeling. He began to share with me how he played football in his high school years. He said that during his freshman, sophomore, and junior years, he ran only 1,800 yards combined. It wasn't until his senior year that he realized there was more inside of him that he needed to tap into in order to make plays on the field, which his physical body alone could not produce. He was held back for the first three years of his football career because he was only functioning from his outward ability—his physical strength. During his senior year, he began to *tell* himself that there was more of him to offer. His performance on the field didn't improve until he believed he could do it and then *told* himself he could. As a result, in his senior year alone, he ran for 1,600 yards. What he ran in three seasons total was nearly matched in one season, all because he got his mind right first, which allowed his physical body to follow.

One thing I have loved in my lifetime is proving people wrong. When the "naysayers" start to talk and doubt me, that's when I am most determined to accomplish the task at hand. Now don't misunderstand me, I don't set out to do just anything that people doubt I can do. What I am speaking of is the dreams and goals that I have decided are a desire of mine to accomplish in my lifetime. When people doubt me and speak against me in those areas, I get a militant mindset about myself and begin to say, "I can do this. I'll prove them wrong." Just hearing myself saying those words has helped me overcome some of the major struggles and challenges I have faced in my life. Every time I would say positive words to myself, my mind was renewed. Most of the time, I would not believe my own words when I said them, but I said them anyway. After I said them repeatedly for long enough, I started to believe in myself. What I discovered was that believing in myself was the key to overcoming every challenge and struggle, and it has been the major element in bringing to pass my desires, goals, and dreams in life. But the key to achieving all of it was to get my mind right first. If one's mind is not thinking positively, one could miss the treasures at their disposal and fail to succeed.

I can recall many times that I have allowed people's negative words to direct my life. People that I did not necessarily know or have any contact with would say things that I allowed to direct my path in life. Then, of course, this made me my biggest critic. I would find myself saying the same things about me as those people had. Let me tell you that when you begin to think and say negative things about yourself, destruction is just around the corner. Not until I chose to get my mind right did I start to see positive changes in my life. I believe that if every young person strives to keep a positive mindset, they will enjoy life more, experience more confidence, and become more successful.

Early Interventions Have Positive Outcomes

I believe that the behavior patterns one is taught and chooses to practice early in life are some of the same ones that the individual chooses to practice for the remainder of their life. Because it is expected that adolescents have a long life ahead of them, learning to discard all the negative and unproductive things society piles upon them is vital for discovering the hidden treasures they possess. In a child's adolescence, there is an unprecedented amount of negative and unwelcome influences that can pile upon their life, and if they don't choose to lay them aside, dig them up, or peel them away, by the time they are in their mid-20s, their life will have accumulated layers upon layers of negativity. If this behavior continues into their 30s and 40s, the weight of life becomes so unbearable that their life can begin to crumble right before their very eyes.

This is why I believe adolescents must learn in their younger years how to stop the cares of society from piling upon them. The treasure within them will be easier to discover if they don't have to peel away years and years of negativity, which has added no value to their life. Just living life is a challenge in itself, but it becomes much more of a challenge when one allows the cares and challenges of society to accumulate, day after day and year after year. You will never be led toward your destiny until you discover the hidden treasures of your soul.

There is greatness stored deep inside every man and woman, boy and girl. For a person to discover that greatness, every individual must change the way he or she thinks. Your mental attitude concerning every situation of life will determine whether you will enjoy the things in life that your hidden treasures were meant to produce. You will never be a productive member of society the way that you were meant to be and desire to be until you discover the treasures of your soul. The sooner young people begin to get a positive mental attitude about their future, the sooner they will start to experience an outward manifestation of what's on the inside.

Children must also have interventions in their lives to combat negative behavior. The longer we wait to intervene when negative behavior begins, the more our children's lives are affected by the negative behavior. When early intervention is neglected, negative behavior can be like cancer or a bad infection spreading in the body. If not treated, negative behavior will continue to spread to other parts of the child's life, influencing their actions, decisions, and lifestyle, and then it will begin to affect others in the home, neighborhood, and community. Failure to intervene early in children's negative behavior patterns affects their decision-making skills, especially in choosing right over wrong, and it also affects how they relate to others. These actions will later lead to further negative actions and outbursts.

My grandmother always kept candy in her purse. As a small boy, I would go to her and stick my hands in her purse without asking. I remember my mother telling my grandmother at some point not to allow me to go into her purse without permission. My grandmother didn't mind my behavior, but my mother knew it was wrong and that it could potentially lead to more serious misbehaviors later. Because my grandmother didn't correct me from the beginning, it led me to think that it was acceptable to go into her purse whenever I felt like it. I later found myself going into the purses of some of my aunts without permission because I was looking for candy. I didn't think of myself as a thief, but I *was* stealing. I went to places I hadn't been invited to and took things that didn't belong to me. It was a negative behavior that, if I had been allowed to continue, could have sent me down a path of greater and more thefts, like stealing cars, home invasions, or other negative behaviors. My mother probably wasn't thinking about these major crimes at that time, but regardless, she knew it was a wrong behavior that needed correction. Just "the look" she gave me, the slap on my hand, or the pointing and waving of the finger was all the intervention needed at my young age. I had learned that these actions were prerequisites to a more serious intervention: spanking.

I believe that many of the crimes that people commit today, and many of the behavior problems we have in our homes, neighborhoods, communities, and schools, are the direct result of negative behaviors that are practiced as a child without early intervention to correct or put a stop to them. Children grow up into young adults thinking it is acceptable to engage in such behaviors if they are not taught right from wrong by receiving early interventions. There is a thin line between being tolerant and patient with adolescents and teens versus becoming a crutch for their negative and unwelcome behaviors. Parents must know when and where to draw that line.

In fact, many parents are held hostage in their own homes because the intervention was ignored or delayed in dealing with their children's negative behaviors earlier in their childhood. Waiting until they are old enough to commit verbal and physical abuse towards the parents is well past due time. It's easy to become a prisoner in their own home. Waiting until the child is in his or her adolescence or teens is much too late. Children need constant reminders from their parents of what is right versus what is wrong. As the saying goes, "If you throw enough mud against a wall some of it is bound to stick".

Directing and teaching children the right way early in life is vital for them to reach their full potential in life. Consider a tree. People plant trees in the ground while the trees are small and young, saplings. Typically, a stick or a straight object is placed in the ground next to the young tree and tied to it to help support the tree and keep it from falling to one side and growing crookedly. If the sapling is left to grow without support, it will grow up leaning to one side or the other, and its root system could be affected by the uneven growth. If the root system does not have a solid foundation, it could affect the whole life of the tree and the fruit it produces. It can cause the tree to be easily uprooted during a storm and even prevent it from producing any fruit at all.

Similarly, children need support from their parents and other authority figures. If they are left to grow without support, they will lean too far in one direction or the other. They will grow up without the root system needed for a balanced, productive life.

How Did We Get Here?

I have said it about my own children and have heard many parents say it about their children too, "Let them learn the hard way." Some parents like to remain silent and not invade their child's space. Their thought process for doing this is that the child will inevitably learn from the experience or learn from some other source. However, being silent will cause you and your child a whole lot of trouble in life. It's true they are learning, but they are learning and making discoveries without guidance or protection. His or her discovery could be fatal without those supports. I believe that many times what causes parents to be silent is the amount of opposition they receive from their children. Some children can be so vocal and strong-willed against their parents' boundaries and rules that the parents stop talking.

Many times, we as parents and leaders go through life with the perception that experience is the best teacher. It's true that experience can and will teach a whole lot, but that doesn't make it the best teacher. Parents and leaders are actually the best teachers. Could it be that this is where part of our problems with rebellious, defiant, and disrespectful teens are birthed from? Could it be that the parents of these children never had a lesson on how to be obedient and show respect? Parents who find themselves in this state should seek to get help with parenting. No child should have to overcome life's obstacles by finding out the hard way. We, as parents and leaders, owe every child the opportunity to live a productive lifestyle with as little trouble as possible.

There was a time in our society when one could see and hear respect without even looking for it. Times have changed. Today, respect must be demanded, and even when it is, most people don't know what it looks like or sounds like. Some people don't know if there is such a thing as respect. I can remember when I was in elementary school and was taught the meaning of respect at the hands of certain teachers. I had one teacher who taught me to recognize respect by using a paddle on my behind. Another teacher taught me how to respect it by pinching the skin of my upper arm and twisting it. Other teachers would use a ruler across the palm of the hand. It might not sound like this could hurt, but it did. Most of all, the message was loud and clear. Today, these techniques would be considered "child abuse," and I am not suggesting that anyone try to gain respect by using these or any other physically or mentally damaging technique.

In the 50s and 60s, the paddle was part of a teacher's learning tools. It was a common thing for a teacher to call a student to the front of the class and demonstrate to him what it meant to have respect in the classroom. Some teachers would use a little tact and take the student into the hallway or other designated places for paddling. Either way, the respect of the student was gained. My teachers would always make sure they followed up the paddling I received with a note home explaining why I had been paddled. The bottom line was that I had shown disrespect toward the teacher and their classroom. The teacher would pin a note on my shirt or place it in my lunch box and instruct me to give it to my parents. I guess I wasn't too bright at a young age, because I did exactly what the teacher told me to do. Today, I think back and ask myself, "Why didn't I just take that note and throw it away? After all, how would my parents know?" No! Being bright or not had nothing to do with it. It was out of honor and respect for my parents that I delivered the note to them because they had taught that to me at home. To tell you the truth, I had a reverent type of fear of my parents.

I know some would argue that respect is earned. If this is where you stand, I totally understand and will agree with you up to a point. It is true that one reaps what he or she sows. With that understanding, if one shows respect, respect is shown in return. The golden rule is, "Do unto others as you would have them do unto you." Ideally, that would always work well, but most people don't think about this in our present-day society.

We live in a time where people are going at a fast pace. It's a time when people have more love for themselves than for their children and fellow people. Many don't respect the constitutional rights of others, yet they demand that their rights not be violated. Many people don't respect the property of others. We live in a society where home invasions are at an all-time high. Businesses are being robbed of their hard-earned dollars. Some people even rob businesses or other establishments seeking drugs and other things of value. We can no longer safely walk down the streets of our neighborhoods and communities without the threat of being mugged, assaulted, or even worse, killed. Little children cannot go outside to play in their own yard without fear of being kidnapped. Many people just don't feel safe anymore. Most don't even know who lives next door to them.

Once, I had a conversation with a man who was seeking help to curb the violence of the teenagers in the town where he lived. He was telling me about the number of children who died in the streets every day from violence. He shared with me how many parents had confessed to him that they feared for their own lives as they walked the streets, and how he would always explain to them that the children creating the violence came from their homes. As I thought more and more about what he had said, it made perfectly good sense. Where else did these children come from, if not from the parents' homes? The children killing one another in outbreaks of street violence came from homes that didn't teach their children the fundamentals of life. They were never taught respect—and consequently, they had no respect to give to the other kids in the streets or to anyone else.

Many home invasions are planned and carried out by the very people who grew up in those same homes. Many homes breed their own criminals who will return one day to commit violence against them. Parents raise children who turn out to be their biggest and deadliest enemies. It is a frightening thought to realize that we as parents could be raising the very thief who will one day victimize us.

If we, as parents and leaders, fail to teach our children the importance of respect while they are young, then it could be our children who later commit violence against us, on our own streets, and in our own homes. They could be the ones who rob the local grocery store, gas station, or bank, all of which are there to serve and support the community we live in. Many times, the children that pollute our streets with drugs and gangs were born and raised in the very houses they are menacing. These children usually become a high risk to society. Many of them will become "repeat offenders" of crime.

Many people have lost all moral character as it relates to respect. If someone wants what you have badly enough, he or she will stop at nothing to get it. Many people are boldly entering places where they are not welcome and taking things that don't rightfully belong to them. Where is the respect for humankind? Where is the respect for the property of others? If it was once there, then how do we get it back? How does one earn respect? How does one earn the right to be respected? The right to be respected is only earned by teaching what respect is, and then by modeling what it looks like, how it acts, and what it says. For example, people that have put in the effort to become law enforcers, judges, doctors, dentists, firemen, pastors, counselors, teachers, administrators, military personnel, and all those who serve in a professional job have earned the right to be respected just by the nature of their training and what that training represents. But how can a child show respect to these people when children are not first required to show respect to their parents or guardians?

Conclusion

Children will have to make some tough choices during their adolescent years. During this time, they will be faced with a multitude of obstacles in their daily life. This is the age when fundamental and long-lasting beliefs and ideas are formed. Our children will make choices based on the things and people they associate with. They will have to go through the "basic training" of becoming an adult, and one day, they will graduate from adolescence to adulthood. But in the meantime, their basic training camp is their home, and their parents run the operations. Parents must keep order and give instructions, rewards, and if needed, correction in the form of discipline.

Children will go through some intense training in the time between adolescence and adulthood. This is the time they really learn about life. It is the parent's responsibility to try and filter out the bad influences and pour in the good, which is not an easy task. But I believe that every parent wants the best for their child, whether they are adolescents or adults. To give their children the best, it is imperative that parents take their position as basic trainers and commanders seriously. Basic training will not last forever. The day will inevitably come when the children will move from the ranks of their home and into the ranks of the world, where an entirely new set of rules and consequences will be waiting for them. How prepared they will be is up to their parents.

Parents must talk with their children about the things they face daily. They must ask hard questions. Two-way communication between the child and parent is essential for a well-balanced relationship. Parents must not be afraid to talk as well as to listen carefully to what their child has to say. As a parent, you just might find out something about your child that you didn't know before.

Parents must take on many roles. They must set examples, teach, direct, lead, support, reward, and discipline. They must deal with social issues that can affect their child. Children are extremely vulnerable when they are left to experience life on their own. Furthermore, parents must be careful and give serious thought to decisions regarding where they allow their children to go and the activities they are permitted to be involved in. Parents have the responsibility to maintain, protect, and educate their children. Parents are obligated and required to provide and take care of their children while they are growing up and going through "basic training." Once basic training is over, the children should be equipped to take care of themselves, confidently and responsibly.

Children will learn about life from someone or something, and if parents fail to teach their children about the world as they see it, then the child will be taught by someone else—perhaps someone they would not approve of. If parents do not lead them, children will seek influence from another source that parents may not agree with, and they may regret not stepping in earlier and taking control. Why not let the training take place at home with the parents as the instructors? Your child will learn the behaviors that you as the parent should be the one to teach. This is the critical time to train your child because once they leave the nest, they are on their own and will start making their own decisions and living life their own way, whether you like it or not.

Coming from a military background, I believe that any organization or individual will fight based on the training received. The family is an organization, and when the children leave home, they are now in hand-to-hand combat with the world; they are going against forces that are designed to destroy them. Lyndon Baines Johnson, the 36th President of the United States, once said, "The family is the cornerstone of our society. More than any other force, it shapes the attitude, the hope, the ambitions, and the values of our child." It's time for parents to join the battle and present their children with knowledge about what is false and what is true. It's time for parents to invest their time in their children and to know all there is to know about their children.

Some people, even some psychologists, believe that educators are the best source for knowing what is going on in a child's life. This is a cultural belief in our society, but it is not the truth. I believe that parents should be the best source for knowing what is going on with our children because parents are the authority figures in the home. If parents are not willing to take authority over their child's life, then someone else will. I agree that teachers and educators are a source, but they shouldn't be relied upon as the best source. Parents should be the first point of reference. They are the "trainers," and the children are the "trainees." Children's success will ultimately be based on what they learn from their parents. Being good parents requires more than just providing food, clothing, and shelter for their children. It also requires protection—as much as possible—from influences that could have a negative impact on the child's life. It requires that children are taught the fundamental principles that will enable them to live a well-balanced, responsible, and productive adult life.

I believe when children are not properly cared for by their parents, they tend to no longer want to live there. This is why many children are running away from their homes and are so-called "divorcing" their parents. They look in places other than their families for security, stability, provision, and love.

Some final words to all adolescents and teens: your parents and your family will be forever, but your friends and associates will come and go. Who do you think is the best teacher for your life?

Some final words to all parents: you and I both will agree that children shouldn't have to suffer because of our mistakes and lack of responsibility and accountability, but we know that many times they do. And we must acknowledge that when they suffer, we hurt too, and often want to give up on them, but we must continue in the things that we know to be moral and right. When we as parents fail to teach our children, we leave them failing in life. It's like a baseball player that never practices hitting the ball. Every time he comes to bat, he strikes out. But the good news is that there is someone out there that understands and can offer you help. You just need to acknowledge that you need help and then accept it when it comes. I am speaking from real-life experiences. There is help available.

Made in the USA
Columbia, SC
16 April 2025

56692780R00050